Not So Simple Just that Easy

JERRY INGRAM

How Faith + Discipline + Perseverance = Prosperity

Not So Simple Just that Easy

TATE PUBLISHING
AND ENTERPRISES, LLC

Published by Tate Publishing & Enterprises, LLC
127 E. Trade Center Terrace | Mustang, Oklahoma 73064 USA
1.888.361.9473 | www.tatepublishing.com

Tate Publishing is committed to excellence in the publishing industry. The company reflects the philosophy established by the founders, based on Psalm 68:11,
"The Lord gave the word and great was the company of those who published it."

Cover design by Rtor Maghuyop
Interior design by Mary Jean Archival

Published in the United States of America

ISBN: 978-1-62295-783-5
1. Religion / Christian Life / Inspirational
12.11.02

Dedication

I dedicate this book to my beautiful wife Katina and our kids for standing by my side and believing in me, giving me the confidence to overcome obstacles in my life. To my mom, June, my brothers, Alton and Jamie, and my sister, Yolanda, I would like to thank you for believing in this book. To my two grandmothers, Gloria, the one living, and Alice, the other who's gone to be with the Lord, and my aunt Kathy, I thank you for your inspiration throughout my life.

To Dr. Tate and the Tate Publishing family, for many books are written, but only a few are chosen. Thank you for your acknowledgement of our Lord and Savior Jesus Christ, who empowers us all, and for believing in this body of work.

Acknowledgements

Scriptures were taken from the following:

King James Version Holy Bible (KJV)
New Living Translation Holy Bible (NLT)
Amplified Bible (AMP)

Contents

Foreword

I to was skeptic about buying books, because I felt like I knew the Holy Bible pretty well and I was somewhat good with scriptures, so I thought to myself, "I don't need to buy any books." I couldn't have been more wrong then the man in the moon (that's an old folk saying).

If I knew so much, then where was I going wrong, I mean think about it, how could any of us know the Holy Bible script for script. So I started reading and to my delight, the more I read different books pertaining to the goodness of God and how Jesus Christ died for you and I, it only reminded me on how to apply what I knew of God's Word and it help me to remember so many different scriptures, that I, to be honest totally forgot about. Remember we all have something to share pertaining to the word of God and the more knowledge and understanding we receive it only blesses and helps us to prosper in life.

For years I struggled with trying to find out what was my purpose in life, not realizing that all I ever wanted to be or accomplished was already in me, I just had to figure out how to unlock those gifts.

I felt as though I had to have a higher education in order to have a great career, then I could be someone looked up to or if I accomplish something with a title, then that would impress others. I grew up knowing that respect was earned not given and the people I seen that had all the respect were people with a title, Doctors, Lawyers, Policemen, Firemen, etc…

I grew up trying to live up to my Grandparents expectations, only to fall short and head in the total opposite direction. Although I grew up in the inner city, I went pretty much too suburban schools from elementary to high school. I thought I had it all together and I was headed somewhere in life.

As I came into adulthood, I gave up that life of being a so called ladies' man and settled down, and now I'm married and have children. I was making pretty nice money from work, it was not my dream job, but it paid the bills. I remember feeling pretty good about myself, not knowing turmoil was right around the corner.

The more money I made the more of a mess I got myself into. I remember experimenting with drugs and alcohol as a teen, but it wasn't that serious, "so I thought," it seemed as though everybody was doing it back then.

As I sunk deeper and deeper into my addiction, I didn't realize how I was suffering and the people in my life that I was hurting, but I never thought it would come to an end. I was making the money so whatever I messed up, I'll have it right back by the end of the week, and besides making money brought me the status, that I thought made me feel good. How selfish of me, and I couldn't believe how far off I was from my upbringing.

Well to make a long story short everything came crumbling down. The house went into foreclosure, I was laid off, and I lost my car as well, but it was at that very moment, after all the things that causes us to go astray, I heard the voice of God and it said to me, "My child, I have loved you since the beginning of time and I will give you all your heart desires if you are willing to let Me be the head of your life."

I wasn't sure if this was the Spirit of God telling me this, because I had done so much that was displeasing to God. I remember the teachings of God's Word when I was little, but could this be that same God my Grandmothers always talked about, could this be God's Holy Spirit, the one that my Mother said I would experience as I went through life, the same God who saved my Mother and blessed her tremendously. I couldn't believe it, but it was true, the same God was willing to accept me, if only I would call on his name.

This was a no-brainer for me; I accepted God's invitation for my life and by me believing, he has blessed me and my family in ways I would have otherwise not understood, but his love for us has no limits.

Friend, God is the answer and Jesus is the way, we all want gratification, possessions, and material things.

This work of art will show you just how to have all you want in life and teach you how to use scriptures that will unlock God's favor in your life and give you the know-how on how to destroy obstacles and the things that separate us from the love of God.

I knew in my heart, if I did not share this book with you, I would be ashamed to call myself a believer. We are supposed to share God's goodness together. I wouldn't be a friend in Christ, if I was to find treasure and not tell you how I did it, so that you may have the same treasures.

Believe in yourself and give God a chance, you have nothing to lose and everything to gain. God will show you things you never imagine.

Introduction

I would like to thank everyone for reading this literature; it is a very special book that deals with principles and the origin of one's true nature. Although at times we are weary, we must be able to channel our inner strength to overcome obstacles that are a part of everyday living. Simultaneously understanding our talents or gifts in order to better not only our lives, but those around us, sufficiently obtaining wisdom in order to help guide others in the way he/she may go, also to gain enough confidence to deal with situations that are overwhelming to one's physical and mental health by maintaining, achieving, and obtaining goals, knowing that God ability's goes beyond our own understanding.

This book confronts the sin in our lives and gives us a sense of direction on how to defeat the unseen forces that plot to steal the joy out of our lives; it also breaks down the delusion that some people have that Lucifer, the devil, who is the enemy of all of us who seek after God, doesn't exist.

Not So Simple Just That Easy asks and gives us the information or blueprint on how we should live our lives according to God's Holy Word and that we get the speck out of our eyes before judging others also to search our hearts to find the love that God put in us from birth as we go forward in our journey as we draw nearer to his divine power.

Each chapter deals with a specific situation or circumstance we may encounter in life and gives hope to the believer, knowing that even though we face obstacles, we can overcome them by trusting in Jesus Christ, who came in the world and died for the sins of humanity.

A life without purpose is folly, but to have purpose in one's life is much gain.

Perseverance through Struggles

There is hope for those of us who choose to walk right and much reward for those of us who stay the course. Many of us know that God is real or exists, but our urge to sin hinders our blessings from God, again acting out our feelings, and we will get into our feelings later in the book, but I too was a person of folly and was chasing the wind.

There was a time in my life when everything that could go wrong did just that. I found myself looking through the glass, facing the mirror, seeing a familiar and not so familiar face staring back. My journey into a life of sin was a harsh one and was about to take center stage. It took me several years to get my act together, but by God's grace, I prevailed.

What is triumph without failure?
What is life without void?
How does one overcome?

For years, I allowed drugs and alcohol to dominate in my life, hoping that neither family nor friends would find out, convincing myself that it would be okay. I was what you would call a closet junky. Sure, I took care of myself, I mean, I wasn't in the streets, looking to party every day or felt like I needed to go get high—no way. Not by any means did I consider that I had a problem as I sunk deeper into my addiction—no way. Would I allow drugs to take me out of character and let my wife and kids see a person who they're not familiar with? No way.

I was under the impression that I had it all together or that all was under control. At first, things couldn't have been better: new baby on the way, new job, bringing home a real nice paycheck every week, feeling like this was it, but when I stopped reading my Bible and spent less time with God, I was pulled in the opposite direction. The partying started increasing, my drug habit got worse, and one drug led to another.

I kept trying to keep my high going. I was blowing money faster than I could make it. The fighting and arguing between my wife and I took a toll on our relationship one fight after another. As I sunk deeper and deeper into the world of drugs and alcohol, I found myself in places that I would never be in if it wasn't for drugs. Lies accumulated more lies; the kids were wondering why Daddy wasn't coming home at night.

I couldn't keep on like this. I was headed nowhere fast. Depression kicked in and thoughts of suicide flowed rapidly as I knew I must face the music the next day or so for I couldn't let my family and friends see me like this.

My wife, kids, mother, grandmother, sister, brother, and aunts, uncle, or coworkers, no way. I would rather jump into a river than for them to see me, how could I keep living this life, how about explaining this to my wife, how could I tell my mother that her oldest son was struggling with drugs and alcohol, no way. But then it happened as I took a free-fall to the bottom. *Boom*! So this is what rock bottom feels like.

The shame I felt and the embarrassment I put my family through, such heartache and pain, a life of turmoil, how could I go on? I thought to myself, maybe this is iniquity passed down through generations to my childhood as I remember being filled with much void and hate. I hated that I couldn't be with my mother or father while other kids were with theirs.

My siblings and I were raised by my great-grandparents until I was the age of twelve, and then finally, we moved in with my mom and stepfather, where I did not stay long, never knowing my father until adulthood. The alcohol and drug use I became accustomed to while my stepfather constantly spiraled out of control, or was it because of the many beatings I took as a little child with an electrical cord by the hands of my great-grandfather?

I wasn't a bad kid; troubled in my spirit, yes, but if you had to deal with what I went through, you too would feel some type of resentment. I ran away from home at the age of twelve, not knowing where I was going to sleep or get food from.

I remember lonely nights, looking for a bridge to sleep under or an abandoned building to camp in just to get away from the elements. I was so afraid and didn't understand why I was going through this. I had so many nights of crying, not knowing where my next meal would come from. No twelve-year-old should have to go through this. This wasn't fair.

How could this be? I was the oldest child. What kind of example would I be to my little sister and brother? I was labeled a runaway for many years and had to grow up way faster than the normal twelve-year-old. I was in adult situations many of times, way too much to handle, but surely, this couldn't be the reason why I stumbled during adulthood, no way.

I was in need of change. I was taught the Word of God as a child. I remember asking God a lot of questions when I was little, not knowing the journey I would take in life would bring me closer to my Redeemer, my road of healing. The process in itself took years, but through this, God would reveal his plan for my life.

How great a God who can take the bad things in our life and turn it around for our good and use what we've been through to help not only you or me in our time of need, but others as well, not understanding that the things that the enemy uses to bring us down, God would use it to lead us to redemption.

The road to redemption was a harsh one, many nights plagued by the symptoms that can bind anyone to addiction. Lost in a wave of sin, not knowing if I had fallen back into this madness of a reality only to awake and realize it was only a dream, thank God.

Through the many trials I had to endure, I persevered because of my willingness to put pride aside and go to God in prayer.

The things we go through in life, I would like to believe, brings us closer to God and gives us the courage and strength to be a blessing to others in their struggles. For how can we tell others about something if we've never been down that road or experienced what they're going through?

To Know Who I Am

Many times in life we second-guess ourselves or regret some of the choices we make, not knowing what's on the other end of that decision, hoping that the decision we've made blossoms into a better circumstance for any of our current affairs or situations.

When in doubt about your ability to understand or make reasonable or responsible decisions in life, we tend to lean on others for advice, which can be helpful at times, or not.

We must learn how to lean not on our own understanding but consider that of a higher power of learning and understanding in order to tackle any obstacles that may be overwhelming to one's physical and mental health.

Every day in life we experience or face problems. Whether at home, work, or just out and about, life has its own way of presenting strange and unfamiliar situations.

To have the ability to recognize things beforehand is the beginning of knowledge, for it is knowledge that keeps us aware and to take notice of situations that occur in life.

Knowledge is used in many forms and fashion, such as being able to heal the sick, building homes and transportation. Also, having knowledge keeps you safe and aware of your surroundings.

Basically, knowledge enables us to apply the necessary skills for any task in life, and with knowledge comes understanding, and with understanding, patience easily follows.

Perseverance comes once we have the ability to understand, the knowledge to know how, and the courage to go forward. I believe the key is to obtain wisdom for wisdom is the root of all achievements.

Wisdom keeps a person from folly. It teaches us about love for one another. Also, it is wisdom that builds the house and understanding that establishes it. Maybe if we took the time to examine our lives according to that which we believe in, we would get a better outlook on what type of people we are or the type we've become.

I know this to be true as well, in that in order to know who we are; we must dig deep within ourselves and search our hearts. It is the heart that determines the character of a person.

Life crisis can also be a determining factor and shape how a person's character develops over time and this is when we must have the knowingness on how not to fall victim to circumstances, but have the confidence in that which one believes in, so we may have the victory over that barrier.

In determining the character, we must understand how feelings work and have the ability to control that most inner part of ourselves.

For example, if someone or something offends you, more than likely you're naturally going to react. This is when your ability to take control of your inner being must take place and then decide what's the best way to resolve this issue.

Now this will determine how far you as an individual have grown and give a good report of your character or just how much more time and space you'll need for improvement.

Know this: no matter how much we think highly of ourselves, test and trials are the formula for building peoples true character, for it's always easier to say than do.

Here's another example: to say you will give to the needy families of this country or the poor children of poverty-stricken countries but never act on those feelings surely leaves room for questioning one's character, not saying or judging in that, we all start out with good intensions, the thing is that we must follow through.

When someone commits a crime, the authorities will try and figure out the character of that individual to get a better understanding of how a person could do such a thing. Just as well when justifying acts and laws of a country, I would like to think that character plays a significant role in doing so.

Speak out to yourself on who you are, speaking on the regular that you're the righteousness of God and no matter what, God loves you.

Well, with that being said, may your character change for the better and blessings fall upon you, as like the rising of the morning sun.

Overcoming the Flesh

People often ask themselves or don't understand some of their actions in life or why the things that we know sometimes to be out of our character we tend to do. This is then followed by a reality check in an individual's physical and mental state of mind.

We need to figure out how to stop the negative ways in our behavior and replace it with the positives.

I've come to the conclusion in that it was not me wanting to do the things which I hated, but it was pleasing my flesh that I allowed to dominate more in me than that which was spiritual. I found myself at a standstill, and that was when I did things of the flesh, I always felt pretty bad afterwards. On the other hand, when I denounced my flesh, I felt enlightened.

My experiences have led me to believe that there are several ways of tackling this issue.

First, acknowledging that there is a problem and that you're very sincere about resolving this important battle and it's a serious battle.

The second thing is finding your inner self or spiritual side and building that part of you up, knowing that your ability to sustain a healthy spiritual balance starts from within.

The third thing is to know that it is okay to fall, but just like in any fall, you pick yourself up, and do not be discouraged.

Remember, the apostles didn't become saints overnight; it took dedication, practice, and time. I love the text where it says, "Ye are of God, little children, and have overcome them because greater is he that is in you than he that is in the world" (1 John 4:4, KJV).

This lets me know that no matter what a person may go through, you can overcome it by believing and trusting on God.

> If we confess our sins, he is faithful and just to forgive us our sins, and to cleanse us from all unrighteousness.
>
> 1 John 1:9 (KJV)

I do know that when you're trying to implement change, many sacrifices have to be made. There are many different ways to be tempted by the flesh, but only one way to overcome it. It's like the old saying, "There are many ways to get into trouble but only one way to avoid it."

We must stay focused on the promise, which is in Christ Jesus, and also, by turning from sin, we gain favor with him who can give us eternal life.

However, the flesh can be very tricky for who can say they will pick up the cross and follow that which they believe and denounce everything they've been accustomed to?

Many times we get sidetracked, and this can cause us to stumble, but if we continue to pursue that which we believe in our hearts, we'll be able to get back up.

We must constantly remind ourselves on a daily basis to fight the good fight, being aware at all times that the enemy never sleeps.

His main objective is to cause us to fall short of the glory of God. I do believe that there are three to four voices we hear in our heads: that of ourselves, the enemy, the voice of God, and his Holy Spirit, but through prayer, obedience, and asking forgiveness of our sins, we can and will prevail.

It's like this, when we empty out the fish tank we have an empty glass container and if we leave that container empty, it will fill up on its own, with dust, cobwebs and corrosion around the edges.

Our Lives, our Human Vessel (Spirit or Soul) is like a fish tank. When we empty out the garbage or the pollution that's in us, we're empty, but what happens when we don't fill back up the tank, it automatically fills up with the things of the world. We need to put back in us clean, pure, the true water of life, so that we stay afloat.

This is another way how the enemy uses our own ability against us and tries to keep his grip on our lives. We must keep feeding ourselves with the Word of God on a consistent basis, not twenty percent to God and eighty percent to the world, but reverse that and you'll definitely see instant progress in your life.

The more you fill up with God's Word; fleshly things will start to decrease, the sinful nature will become less attractive and a New Beginning will be unlocked for you.

Remember what the scripture tells us.

> So put to death the sinful, earthly things lurking within you. Have nothing to do with sexual immorality, impurity, lust, and evil desires. Don't be greedy, for a greedy person is an idolater, worshiping the things of this world. Because of these sins, the anger of God is coming.
>
> Colossians 3:5–6 (NLT)

Also, know that God loves those who love him; he guides and protects those who follow after his righteous ways.

May his splendid power reveal itself to you as you learn to trust and lean on his unfailing love?

Afraid

First, we start with understanding the definition of afraid, which is the mental state ruled by fear or the belief that something or someone is dangerous.

I would like to believe that we were given a spirit not of fear, but that of a conqueror's, for the land was given to man to rule over it and replenish it as well.

> For God has not given us the spirit of fear but of power, and of love, and of a sound mind.
>
> 2 Timothy 1:7 (KJV)

We must learn to overcome fear for it can lead us to destruction, for it is fear that separates us from one another. It's also fear that keeps us in bondage; it is fear that causes men to war against each other. Also, fear destroys our inner being.

In order to go forward in life, we must know how to separate from the stronghold of fear and stop letting this symptom have dominion over our lives.

Confidence can be a way of overcoming fear, but how does one gain confidence?

Confidence comes by having a firm belief in oneself or assurance, which is the basic meaning of certainty and means sureness of oneself and lack of fears or doubts about your abilities.

Here are some examples: if King David was afraid, he would have never defeated Goliath when he was an adolescent in biblical history.

Christ had the confidence in dying for us all, so that our sins would be forgiven, in order for us to gain everlasting life through Him with God.

I do know this: once fear has consumed you, your inner being starts to lose all control, sending shock waves throughout your body, destroying any logical answer that would, in other words, help you to overcome your situation.

Most of the time, fear is brought on us by some of the choices we make or our actions, and other times, we have no control of it. For example, if a loved one has been hurt in an accident, someone burglarizes your home or place of business; all these are things or situations not of your control.

With that being said, let's examine some common fears and see how we can break down the strongholds, anxiety attacks, nervousness, and phobias in our lives.

These are all symptoms of fear or being afraid, but if we could start to tame our minds on how to react to fear and know that fear is a spirit that eats away at our structure and understand that it works off of our feelings, we can overcome it, for God did not give us a spirit of fear but of power and of love and of a sound mind.

If we operate in God, he has promised the believer that fear will never have dominion over him. Just think how God, his light, shined through the darkness.

> In the beginning God created the heaven and the earth and the earth was without form, and void; and darkness was upon the face of the deep. And the Spirit of God moved upon the face of the waters. And God said, let there be light and there was light. And God saw the light, that it was good: and God divided the light from the darkness.
>
> Genesis 1:2–4 (KJV)

> Remember, Jesus saith unto him, I am the way, the truth, and the life: no man cometh unto the Father but by him.
>
> John 14:6 (KJV)

To Know I'm Not Alone

Many times in life, we feel as though we're all alone and no one cares about what we're going through and that our circumstance is greater than what we perceive it to be, but if we knew that there is a solution to defeating what may feel like an unbearable challenge that appears to be eating away at our souls, that would make all the difference.

Remember, challenges come our way every day, but all thanks unto God, who through Jesus Christ gives us strength and to know that we are more than conquerors.

We all know that life can seem to deal you a bunch of challenges at one time. The loss of employment, deteriorating health, foreclosure on your home, can all cause physical and mental stress.

I remember when I was about twelve years of age and I was riding my bike down the sidewalk and before I knew it, here came this dog out of nowhere and started chasing me, so my first reaction was to get away from what I perceived to be a threat, not knowing that I was about to be hit by a car and cause myself even greater pain.

All I remember was hearing a loud thump, my head shattering the car windshield as I lay in an unconscious state of mind. When I came to, I felt so much pain and all alone and felt as though I was going to die due to the head injury I suffered. Little did I know that I was not alone, and God had spared my life? He gave his holy angels charge over my well-being.

I'm truly thankful for God saving and preserving my life many of times. Remember, God chose us, for we turned from God in ignorance and disobedience, but through Jesus Christ, he forgives us our sins and loves us eternally.

> For God so loved the world, that he gave his only begotten Son, that whosoever believeth in him should not perish, but have everlasting life. For God sent not his Son into the world to condemn the world; but that the world through him might be saved.
>
> John 3:16–17 (KJV)

Now let's talk about pride, which can get in the way of us reaching out to others in our time of need, when actually, we all need a shoulder to lean on sometimes.

I found myself at a standstill, not reaching out to others in my time of need, because I was so worried about what others might say or think about me.

I always comforted everyone else and was so ashamed to express to anyone about what I was going through. I then started to dig deep within myself and rely on a higher power.

I began to read scriptures and found out that I'm not alone and that God does hear me and loves me. This was the beginning of a beautiful relationship, one I never dreamt of having on this magnitude.

I now know his love for me, and there is no more being prideful in me for his Word has given me a new understanding in life, and it's not only for me but for us all.

Just think, it's good to know that we have someone in high places looking out for us; all we need to do is believe he died for us and call on his name. Jesus, Jesus, Jesus.

How to Love and Be Loved

Love, what a beautiful word, for it was love that saved us from destruction, for it is love that keeps us safe in his arms.

To love is to open oneself or inner being to affections that allow the heart to have feelings toward or subject to an individual or thing.

We sometimes find ourselves hard to love. This could be from various reasons, things such as a lonely past, betrayal, and the insensibility to understand and identify with others, as well as yourself, on how to open or express what you feel.

The first jewel is allowing you to be open-minded to love.

Take a husband and wife, the blueprint to their marriage working is trust, for it's trust that allows us to open up to each other. The same goes for any relationship we have with other family members and friends.

Remember, for it was out of love that Christ died for us, knowing that we would stumble, yet trusting that we would live accordingly to the Father's perfect will.

Love fills the heart with joy, and there is no sorrow in joy.

I love what the scripture says, "Give thanks to the Lord, for he is good! His faithful love endures forever" (Psalm 136:1, NLT). What a factual statement.

When examining your feelings, you should always submit yourself to understanding what it is you feel and why you feel a certain way. Once you have the ability to take control of your inner being, or in this case, your feelings, you'll see that it is easier to love than you think.

Love can be dissected in many different forms, but it all falls back to one simple rule, which is opening your heart and knowing that God is love and we being sculpted in his image were formed in God's perfect love.

To Know My Purpose

I believe that there are different ways of living; one is that we are living just to die and another is living with a purpose for it is foolish just to be living to die for there is no joy in people dying without believing in him who died for us and was resurrected so as we shall be in the latter days.

Take oxygen for an example; it is without color or odor, yet its sole purpose is to help humans, animals, and other species and things to live.

Here's something, did you know that without oxygen, fire could not burn. The same as with human life; to not have purpose is to be dead to life.

Its purpose that gives us the motivation to achieve any success in life, which leads me to believe, to gain much wealth here on earth and leave it all behind is useless. We can say we want to obtain wealth so we may leave it for our children when we pass away, but actually, we would like to be here to enjoy it with them.

So what is it to gain much wealth and lose it all in the end; this I could not understand, "know this?"

> The horse leach hath two daughters, crying, Give, give. There are three things that are never satisfied, yea, four things say not, it is enough: The grave, and

> the barren womb, the earth that is not filled with water; and the fire that saith not, it is enough.
>
> Proverbs 30:15–16 (KJV)

And these all have purpose, so how much more we being human beings, who possess the land, should have purpose in our lives?

We need to start examining what we seek in life and line up our lives in agreement with scripture.

I've found this to be true in most cases, and that is whatever we put out is what we get in return.

For example, we've all heard that when an individual does anything wrong, there are consequences for their actions, and we who are quick to judge might say, "Well, that's what they get." And that is the wrong way of thinking, but you see how your output will affect your input. If you put out positive energy and surround yourself around positive people, then in return, positive things will happen for you and your loved ones; the same goes with a surrounding of negativity.

If someone sets a goal in their life, let's say to become a doctor, lawyer, postal worker, police officer, or even a pastor of a church, the first thing to do is to refrain from negative thinking because we all at times can get discouraged and feel this is just too much. And trust me, I do understand. Before becoming a writer, I had to ask God to give me the courage to believe in myself, and then hope someone else would see that potential in what God was doing in my life by using the gift of words.

Some believe that our lives were preordained; maybe this could be true, but I would also like to believe that we have the choice to decide what we are destined to become.

Having purpose fulfills the soul for it gives us the drive to go forward, and without it, there is no determination to make anything of our lives. I don't know anyone who doesn't want to have success or be well off enough to take care of their family.

Remember, applying purpose in our lives opens the door on a whole new understanding of living.

May you experience God's peace, which exceeds anything we can understand?

Overcoming Addictions

People hate to discuss their addictions for we all hate to admit we're addicted to anything. The word itself sounds bad, addicted. This can be a touchy subject.

In any case, an addiction is a condition of being a slave to a habit and can be unhealthy to a person's health. A habit is often an unconscious pattern of behavior that is acquired through frequent repetition.

It's never easy to kick bad habits, and it requires strength from within. It also may require help from others who've been down that path.

It really takes a person to be fed up and want to change. If you're not absolutely sure or have a positive attitude, there will be no change, and you may find yourself asking if change is possible.

Some addictions can cause friction between family and friends and can drive any normal human insane or cause some to commit suicide, God forbid. We must stay alert to what it is that causes us to return to our old ways and find a system or program that can help us overcome any addiction that exists or any we pick up along the way.

There are so many things a person can be addicted to that I can't even attempt to name them all.

The first step to overcoming is realizing that there is something that is keeping you in bondage.

Secondly, is to avoid the things or people which trigger you and mislead you into opening that door again or going back down that old familiar path, which leads to destruction.

It's so easy to say we won't do that again and then find ourselves right back doing that which we swore we wouldn't do.

I'm reminded of a scripture in the Holy Bible about the teachings of the Apostle Paul and that is "For that which I do, I allow not; for what I would, that do I not; but what I hate, that do I" (Romans 7:15, KJV).

Life can be puzzling at times, but we must not succumb to the things that work against us.

Thirdly, I've found that resorting to a greater power (God) other than ourselves can be a major step in the right direction.

I've always found it to be very helpful when I didn't look to my own understanding, but that in which I believe.

The fourth thing is once you've sustained the ability to move forward, you must remind yourself constantly to stay on course and be obedient to that which you are trying to accomplish.

In order for this to work and whenever we sway to the left or the right, this is when we must catch ourselves and say to yourself, I will not be misled, for I know where this leads.

It is very important that we continue to fight the good fight.

> For though we walk in the flesh, we do not war after the flesh, for the weapons of our warfare are not carnal, but mighty through God to the pulling down of strongholds, casting down imaginations and every high thing that exalteth itself against the knowledge of God, and bringing into captivity every thought to the obedience of Christ.
>
> 2 Corinthians 10:3–5 (KJV)

This is one particular scripture that helps me in my day-to-day walk in Jesus; also, he has given us the instructions on defeating every obstacle in our lives. As we put God first and walk in his perfect love, so shall we reap all that God has to give.

Wisdom and the Renewing of the Mind

When I think of Wisdom, I think of Elegance, Splendor, Kings, and Queens, but truly, what is wisdom and how is it different from knowledge and understanding, or are they one in the same?

How does one obtain wisdom and are there different types of wisdom?

This I do know: "Only by pride cometh contention; but with the well advised is wisdom" (Proverbs 13:10, KJV). So you ask yourself again, what is wisdom? Wisdom is having the ability to make good judgment, or based on the experience one may have, to make sound judgment in every aspect of your life. So in contrast, wisdom comes by having knowledge and understanding for one can't operate without the other for who can understand anything if you have no knowledge of it?

King Solomon asks God to please make him wise and teach him the difference between right and wrong. Then he would know how to rule over God's people. The Good Book also tells us of the story of King Solomon:

> Then came there two women, that were harlots, unto the king, and stood before him; And the one

women said, O my Lord, I and this women dwell in one house; and I was delivered of a child with her in the house. And it came to pass the third day after that I was delivered, that this women was delivered also: and we were together; there was no stranger with us in the house, save we two in the house. And this woman's child died in the night; because she overlaid it. And she arose at midnight, and took my son from beside me, while thy handmaid slept, and laid it in her bosom, and laid her dead child in my bosom. And when I rose in the morning to give my child suck, behold it was dead: but when I had considered it in the morning, behold, it was not my son, which I did bear. And the other women said, Nay; but the living is my son, and the dead is thy son. And this said, no; but the dead is thy son, and the living is my son. Thus they spoke before the king.

1 Kings 3:16–22 (KJV)

Then said the king, the one saith, this is my son that liveth, and thy son is the dead: and the other saith: nay; but thy son is the dead, and my son is the living. And the king said, bring me a sword. And they brought a sword before the king. And the king said, divide the living child in two and give half to the one, and half to the other. Then spake the woman whose the living child was unto the king, for her bowels yearned upon her son, and she said,

> O my Lord give her the living child and in no wise slay it. But the other said, let it be neither mine nor thine, but divide it. Then the king answered and said, give her the living child, and in no wise slay it: she is the mother thereof. And all Israel heard of the judgment which the king had judged; and they feared the king: for they saw that the wisdom of God was in him, to do judgment.
>
> 1 Kings 3:23–28 (KJV)

We must get our hearts right, for some believe the heart is the strongest muscle in our mortal bodies. Whatever the case, I do know that what's in a person's heart, that will he or she do.

Remember, we are judged by what is in our hearts for the heart plays a big role in developing and shaping our character. Also, as you awake in the morning, remember to arise with God in your heart.

This leads me to the next topic: the renewing of our minds. The renewing of the mind must take place if wisdom is to ever come and sit with us or dwell in us.

The old conversations, the old friends, and things of our past that we seem to venture back to every now and then, our words and our actions must come in agreement to the Word of God. If it doesn't, then we have no need for it.

In the New Testament, the Bible says this:

> What sorrow awaits the world, because it tempts people to sin. Temptations are inevitable, but what

> sorrow awaits the person who does the tempting. So if your hand or foot causes you to sin, cut if off and throw it away. It's better to enter eternal life with only one hand or foot than to be thrown into eternal fire with both of your hands and feet. And if your eye causes you to sin, gouge it out and throw it away. It's better to eternal life with only one eye than to have two eyes and be thrown into the fire of hell.
>
> Matthew 18:7–9 (NLT)

Thank God he doesn't ask us to do away with our brains. We really would be in trouble, but he does tell us to renew our minds by keeping pollution or garbage out.

We must train our mind to focus on the goodness of the Lord; again, this process must be repeated daily, over and over again until it becomes natural to us.

Scripture says,

> That ye put off concerning the former conversation the old man, which is corrupt according to deceitful lusts; And be renewed in the spirit of your mind; and that ye put on the new man, which after God is created in righteousness and true holiness.
>
> Ephesians 4:22–24, (KJV)

Why Am I Not Advancing?

Ask yourself how advancement comes about. In life, whether it is success on the job, love life, or spirit life, none of this can be accomplished unless the three factors are applied. I call them DHWB. Dedication, hard work, and believing in your ability or talent that God has given you are the key factors in advancing.

Some say you're lucky when good fortune happens to you, or instead of being lucky, they say it's when hard work meets opportunity. I, on the other hand, from a spiritual standpoint, would call it being blessed, for anything a man receives that's good on this earth comes from above.

I know this to be true because of my experiences. Also, the Good Book tells us, "Every good gift and every perfect gift is from above, and cometh down from the Father of lights, with whom is no variableness, neither shadow of turning" (James 1:17, KJV).

The good thing about God is that we're not under any obligation. He puts no pressure on us; he gives us the chance to choose freely. We're the ones that determine which road to take in life. Even if we take the wrong road, the Father still gives us the opportunity to turn our lives around by us sincerely coming to him in prayer and repentance and asking for forgiveness from God, who searches the hearts of us all.

I quote the scripture once again so you may get this down in your spirit.

> If we confess our sins, he is faithful and just to forgive us our sins, and to cleanse us from all unrighteousness.
>
> 1 John 1:9 (KJV)

The things we do today will determine our outcome in the future. Bad company or wrong decisions can hinder the growth of advancement as well as cause us to drift along time after time.

I've always known that if we put God first, the same we can expect in return, and he will always give us a clear view on how to be productive and better in life, period.

Understanding Signs

Let's start off by determining what signs are. Signs are usually referred to as marks, symbols, or figures. They also can be used as warnings or as a way of conveying information. I believe that signs are definitely helpful.

Signs can be acknowledged by a person having the ability to tap into a greater source of understanding and knowledge, or as some would think, reading between the lines. But I would like to believe it's a little more to it than that.

Being able to read signs spiritually is a special gift, and once unlocked, a greater power of sensibility is given to the beholder. Also, being able to read signs can save lives and work miracles in people's lives, and for those of us who are blessed enough to tap into the spiritual realm, things can and will be unlocked to you like never before.

I think about how I go about my day and the times when I read something or ask God about how I should respond to something that either happened to me or about someone I talk with. Well, somehow, God would always give me confirmation on how to approach any situation, whether through reading his Word, watching television, listening to the radio, or just a feeling in my spirit, which I knew was of God's Holy Spirit.

In the natural, I wouldn't have caught it or have been able to read or hear the signs, but by spending time with God, indulging in his Word, I was able to pick it up. The same goes for any of us who spend time in His Word, the more we become in tune to hearing the voice of God, which is his Holy Spirit, the clearer the picture for our lives becomes.

I was at work one day and overheard one of my coworkers talking bad about another coworker, and it angered me to see this guy talking bad about my friend because I thought we were on the same team. Not thinking, I spoke out and said, "What is your problem?"

The proper thing to do would have been to confront him in love, knowing that it was not him that was actually saying all this bad stuff, but the enemy or forces that were not of God.

That was one of the times I missed the sign, but don't beat yourself over the head like I did, for God knows we're not perfect but are of flesh. This is why Jesus paid the ultimate price for you and me, because he who is perfect knew we would fall, but through Jesus, the only begotten son of the Father, we have hope and a connection to God.

Staying Focus

Anything in life can be hard to do if there is no drive or motivation. What are you working toward?

I've found that, in my own personal experiences, taking time out for you can relax the mind. Meditation and focusing on your inner being can be very helpful.

For some people, focusing on just one thing can be boring or time-consuming and takes a great deal of concentrating because it's so easy to get distracted, and it seems to be complicated to stay on course. You must embrace the uplifting of the spirit of God, which is the Holy Spirit.

> The (enemy) thief cometh not, but for to steal, and to kill and to destroy: I am come that they might have life, and that they might have life more abundantly.
>
> John 10:10 (KJV)

Remember, stay in the fight; storms are trouble, and troubles don't last always. After the rain, everything starts to clear up, and never forget that at the end of every tunnel there is light.

I wish I knew what I know now, in that when I would take one step forward, it took the ability to channel all of my strength in that direction. Also, when I would lose focus, it was like taking ten steps backward.

I felt as though my world was crumbling all around me. I then started questioning my ability to move forward in life, and I was not able to comprehend what was happening to me.

Why can't I stay focused enough to get control of my life, and what was I doing wrong? I felt like a failure, how, could someone have so much potential and not know what to do with it. It was like fighting a lost cause, and then I felt like maybe if I talked to someone or tried therapy, I would be better.

I've come to the conclusion and that by seeking God's advice has help me truly get a grip on life. Sure, going to therapy or talking with family and friends was good, but I still felt incomplete.

> For, I'm reminded of the words of the believer; Ye are of God, little children and have overcome them: because greater is he that is in you than he that is in the world.
>
> 1 John 4:4 (KJV)

This gives me confidence in that I'm not a failure and was blessed from above with the ability to stay focused and receive the promise, which is in Jesus Christ.

I do believe that nothing happens overnight only that of the unexpected and if we stay true to our faith or cause in which we believe everything else will fall in place and knowing that the words of God are basic instruction for our everyday lives.

Why Do Things Bother Me So Much?

Ask yourself, why do things bother any of us so much? We all are faced with difficult decisions in life.

There is always something that gets on your last nerve, such as someone cutting in and out of traffic or jumping in your lane, not getting off from work on time, or something as small as the kids not cleaning up after themselves when fixing a sandwich or meal. Here's a good one—not keeping their room clean. All of these things can drive any normal person to their breaking point.

We must learn how not to react in a negative way when things are out of line and try channeling that energy and turning it into a positive reaction, and trust me, I know how hard that can be for some of us. I found that in most of my situations, I would overreact and let my emotions run wild and would later find myself facing the mirror, wondering, was that me.

We must understand that things can only get to us if we allow it, and the less time we spend thinking about something, the less it bothers us. Vice versa, the more we feed into it, more than likely, we're going to get upset or angry.

Focusing on the good and not the bad or what somebody may have said to offend you or something someone has done to you will pass, knowing that tears come and go, and time heals all wounds.

I'll give you an example: remember when you're at work and can't wait to get off/clock out and your mind has homed in on the clock and it's like the time can't turn 4:00 p.m. fast enough, and you and I know, the longer you stare at that clock, the slower the time goes, but if you concentrate on finishing up your task or even helping someone else with theirs, the time will pass, and you'll be home before you know it, and then watch how fast time really passes, and before you know it, you'll be right back at work the next day, ready to do it all over again.

It's funny how on one hand it seems as though time goes slow and on the other it's fast, but in actuality, I believe time hasn't moved any faster or slower than it always has.

I've always considered the three-step rule:

1. Always remain calm.
2. Turn a negative into a positive (and this is as simple as sixth-grade math).
3. Focus on something or someone who made you smile or happy thoughts.

Now, once all three steps have been integrated, you've now applied smarts over ignorance. Congratulations. Give yourself a pat on the back. It's just that simple. It took me a while to get it, but I got it.

Thank God for his patience, which in return has taught me patience?

With anything in life, having a routine and practicing it over and over so that it becomes second nature will help you to become more sufficient in winning the battles.

Obedience/Discipline

Although two different words, neither can work without the other, for there can be no obedience without discipline and no discipline without obedience.

Let's examine that a bit further. We know that obedience is the act of doing what one is told or the submission to authority or law. Now, with that in mind, let's breakdown discipline or give its meaning and how it relates to obedience, which is to train or bring to a condition of order and obedience also the training of the mind or character.

In order for change to come in our life, we must yield to the knowledge of obedience and the understanding on how to discipline our mind and mortal bodies.

For a man gains favor from God's grace, and doors are opened by being obedient to that which is true, which is in Jesus Christ, and truth comes by studying and believing in that which was in the beginning and then manifested in the flesh, which died for our sins and has risen and shall return for all of us who have kept his Word and lived our lives accordingly.

Disciplining ourselves to the Word of God is a for sure way on God moving on our behalf.

Discipline starts by changing the way we think, talk, and behave, for no one can say he or she is a new person if these three very important components haven't been renewed.

It is never easy disciplining ourselves for its human nature to want. I remember trying to lose weight and how hard it was to discipline myself to change my bad eating habits, and on top of that, develop some type of training exercise.

I found out that I was unable to keep on track and maintain a healthy diet in order to lose the weight. I believe we are only in the position we're in because of the lack of obedience and discipline in our lives.

When we don't acknowledge our power we possess in Jesus Christ, we fall short every time, but when we apply the tools in which God has bestowed upon us, victory is ours.

Always remember that obedience comes by constantly reminding ourselves to stay focused on our God-given ability, so that we are able to access the knowledge of God as we discipline ourselves in every aspect of life.

Stepping into the Light

Why must we be slaves to our bodies, our minds, and our feelings? Shouldn't it be the other way around, in that our body, mind, and feelings are in submission to that individual to whom they belong?

We must take the blinders off or the shield that has kept us hidden from discovering who we really are, stepping out of the darkness, which keeps us in turmoil, and cleansing ourselves with the word of truth so that we may step into a new light. Well, some may say, how does, one receive the light?

The first thing is to acknowledge that Jesus Christ is the son of God, who came into the world and died for our transgressions.

> But he was wounded for our transgressions, he was bruised for our iniquities: the chastisement of our peace was upon him; and with his stripes we are healed.
>
> Isaiah 53:5 (KJV)

The only way to the Father is through the blood of Jesus Christ. Know this, the enemy and the wicked forces of this world know that through the blood of Jesus, we have victory and that the adversaries of God are defeated.

We must start the process of tapping into God's unlimited source of divine power, which he has offered to us all.

I'm reminded of the scripture.

> Finally, my brethren, be strong in the Lord, and in the power of his might. Put on the whole amour of God that ye may be able to stand against the wiles of the devil. For we wrestle not against flesh and blood, but against principalities, against powers, against the rulers of the darkness of this world, against spiritual wickedness in high places. Wherefore take unto you the whole armour of God that ye may be able to withstand in the evil day, and having done all to stand. Stand therefore having your loins girt about with truth, and having on the breastplate of righteousness; and your feet shod with the preparation of the gospel of peace; above all, taking the shield of faith, wherewith ye shall be able to quench all the fiery darts of the wicked. And take the helmet of salvation, and the sword of the spirit, which is the word of God: Praying always with all prayer and supplication in the spirit, and watching thereunto with all perseverance and supplication for all saints.
>
> Ephesians 6: 10–18 (KJV)

This is the blueprint for stepping into the light and staying on course and finishing and with that being said, we must learn to be truthful, help others in their time of need, resist temptation, and go to God with anything that troubles us, and everything will fall in place.

Here is a prayer I say every day, sometimes two or three times a day.

Lord watch over my Family and I, protect us, guide us, cleanse us, heal us and help us to prosper in you, Lord, in the natural and the super natural and may we always remember to put you first in all that we do, continually walking in your love and trusting all of our cares unto you.

Amen, Amen, Amen.

May you prevail in your new life through our Lord Jesus as you begin to accept God's love in your life, while being blessed and a blessing to those you have lost their way?

Why Me

We often ask ourselves this question a lot. The truth is why any of us.

Why do we go through so much?

We all are bothered by troubling times, but must fight through the storms, giving God praise when it's good times and bad.

We now know that life's problems can occur when we least expect them and can really tear us down. Do you ever notice that when things go wrong, they always take place at the wrong time? But then again, when is it ever a good time for things to go wrong? I find myself dealing with issues far greater than my ability to control, or at least I thought.

In my spiritual walk, I've struggled with staying with it or staying on track and would find myself doing good for a while, and then it happens. Just when I thought I've got everything under control, I allow myself to stumble, not God, not the enemy, but me, by allowing myself to listen to the tricks of the enemy for I could have blocked the influences of the enemy by bringing those negative things or whispers into the obedience of Christ.

It's like walking down the street and I know there is trouble up ahead, but I continue to keep going in that direction.

Or here is another example: To be driving on the highway and I'm going to get off at the next exit, but there's a sign that says that the exit is closed, and I try and get off at the exit anyhow, knowing the sign just said that the exit was closed, so then it's not God nor the enemy, but my lack of obedience. So is the same with our walk in the Lord. We allow ourselves to be tricked, maybe not so much directly, but indirectly, right back into that old, familiar situation.

Remember this; the scripture reads like this.

> Watch and pray that ye enter not into temptation: the spirit indeed is willing, but the flesh is weak.
>
> Matthew 41:26 (KJV)

This lets me know that even though I may have good intensions, there is still the opportunity to get sidetracked, but thanks be unto God for there is no problem or situation that Christ hasn't already overcome.

We shall have victory, believe it, and receive it, because it is already done.

Focusing Energy

Whatever or wherever you put or direct your energy, whether good or bad, that is where you're most likely to succeed. Good energy seems as though it's hard to constantly maintain, while bad energy is so easy to succumb to.

There are many ways we can channel our energy or release it. When you feel overwhelmed with things in life, say work, learning a new trade or subject, and let's say motherhood, you must know how to change up.

Change up by simply not focusing so hard on any one thing or situation, but being able to release, then breathe, take a step back so that you don't faint or give up on that which you are doing.

I feel as though for some people taking a walk through the park or exercising can definitely help out a whole lot. I also believe that prayer is a good way of focusing energy and helping anyone keep their sanity.

Remember, and I reiterate, it's always easier to say than to do, so our doing should be as quick as our saying, and then, and only then, will we see results. We must never tarry in trying to succeed.

It's okay to get frustrated; that's normal. But never decide to give up on life for the end can be swift.

If you focus your energy on being mean or always talking bad about others, does it really make you feel good? I would like to think not, but if you could focus that energy on being good or being a person of compassion, you would see how much time you've wasted being miserable and focusing your energy on being bad.

However you decide to use your energy, know that it not only affects you, but those around you as well. I end with this, and ask how we can be a people of one nation and not care for others.

The Discussion

We're not perfect; if we were, there would be no need for the one which is perfect.

When presidents or government fails us, should we rush into judgments?

When family fails?

When friends are nowhere to be found?

There is one who we can surely count on, and his name is Jesus. I say, we must not count ourselves to be perfect, and if blessed with the ability or skills that others lack, whether it's a professional athlete, celebrity, or a person of high office, you should never look down on anyone.

If we say we love God, then it should be reflected in the way we carry ourselves and our discussions.

For we all have fallen short of his glory.

I say this; does a person choose to be sick? How about being poor? I would hope not, God forbid, so how much more those of us who have been blessed with our health, our finances, should help those in need, our reward is not from man, but in heaven.

We are all special in God's eyes.

Take the animals of this world—they live on instinct, but we live by choice, and as we make the transition into becoming what God has for us, then it becomes clear to us, that we live by faith. This lets me know that we all were put here to be great.

We've all made mistakes and are going to make many more, but its love in a person that other people can connect to. God still has faith in humanity, but it starts with us as individuals in walking in that love, which is activated through Jesus Christ.

Let's stop being so quick to judge and be more watchful of how we treat each other. If we must judge, let it start with ourselves.

> So when they continued asking him, he lifted up himself, and said unto them, He that is without sin among you; let him first cast a stone at her.
>
> John 8:7 (KJV)

Life and the Fulfillment Of

Strange, life, the things we go through, the obstacles we face, the people we meet, the changing of the seasons, the maturity of adulthood, the difference in beliefs of cultures, the way of the world. I often wonder in life, am I destine to be or is it my destiny to become someone great in this life.

They say life is what we make it to be, but is that really true? For I've known people who just couldn't catch a break.

Shades of darkness, rays of light, both have purpose in the fulfillment of life. No one knows which way the wind blows nor can we see it, but we all know it exists.

I too am a person of conscience, so it bothers me greatly to know that everything has an end.

The rain flows from above and then stops.

The sun returns from whence it came. Life itself comes to an end, and the world as we know it will cease to exist one day.

Why is it that some can gain a whole lot and others so little?

What is healing without suffering, joy without pain? If there was no death, would we really appreciate life?

So many questions, but only one way to receive the answers we seek.

As we spend time with God, seeking a personal relationship with him and indulging ourselves into his Holy Word, knowing that by practicing and implementing God's perfect will for our lives, so shall we be blessed, in our homes, our workplace, in our health, our finances, our children shall be blessed as well, ultimately achieving the goal, which is our reward in heaven.

Finally seeing the face of him who died for you and me, our Lord and Savior, Jesus Christ.

Activating Your Gifts

I'm always reminded of the story of David and how he conquered the giant, Goliath. I understand now why no one but David, the shepherd boy, could conquer the giant.

The things we face in life, sometimes, and I repeat are out of our control and at other times are self-inflicted.

We must learn to face our fears head-on and trust in him who gives us the strength to conquer all, knowing that he is faithful enough to see us through. We must be able to defeat the Goliaths in our lives, and as we do so, we will see the power of God manifest itself in us.

Remember, faith overcomes fear, and once we as believers start activating our gift, which is our faith in Jesus Christ, fear has to go.

Young David had faith in God, and by having so, he was able to activate his gift, which gave him the strength and courage to defeat Goliath. If God gave the young shepherd boy, David, the ability to defeat Goliath, won't he do the same for you and everyone else?

For God's Word says, "Jesus Christ is the same yesterday, today, and forever" (Hebrews 13:8, NLT).

Once David was able to overcome his fear by activating his faith in God, he became a champion; victory was his for the taking.

When David learned to walk in faith, God was now ready to use him, and thus sparks the story of the mighty King David.

Everyone has their own path to travel; we all have our own cup to bear. Why go through life all alone when God promises to help us through it all?

I believe that God allows us to go through things in life to help us come into his understanding.

For surely, who could say they would call on God's name if everything was just handed to them?

I believe that God does use our situations or circumstances to draw us near to him. It gives me much joy to know that someone like me can be close to God by opening up my heart and receiving all that God has to offer. There is much satisfaction and relief in my spirit as I walk in God's love.

I now know that as believers of God, if we would just learn to walk in faith, he will not only direct our paths, but lead us to fulfill our destiny. For God wishes for all to be saved and that none should perish.

When we start to walk in faith, we become new creatures, former things are passed on, and we possess the light, which through Christ Jesus conquers any darkness in our life.

Therefore if any man be in Christ, he is a new creature: old things are passed away; behold all things are become new. 2 Corinthians 5:17 (KJV)

Words of the Wise

It's not in God's will to conceal things from us, but until we are ready to receive it, then and only then will we know God's plans for our life. It is a privilege to even be considered, to be called a brother or sister of Jesus Christ for if God was to reveal his plans for our lives, I mean, think about it, how can we accept God, when we're not walking in his love? Know this, the understanding of God goes way beyond that of what we could ever begin to understand.

God does allow us or gives us access to him through his Holy Word by way of Jesus to understand how to live our lives while here on earth and, most importantly, life after with him.

> Does anyone know, no one can comprehend the height of heaven, the depth of earth, or all that goes on in the king's mind.
>
> Proverbs 25:3 (NLT)

> Remove the impurities from silver, and the sterling will be ready for the silversmith.
>
> Proverbs 25:4 (NLT)

Remove wickedness from your heart, and you shall be made whole or purified. Never make yourself out to be more than what you are and never claim to know more than what you really know, lest you be called upon and not have the answers that others seek; save yourself the embarrassment.

Always remember to get the facts straight before opening your mouth lest you be called a gossiper and never regain your good reputation back. Always put God first. Rise in the morning, giving him praise. No matter what, God still loves you.

We feel sometimes as though God lets us down; we feel as though no matter how hard we try to do things that honor him, nothing comes about.

I know this pain often too well. What's the meaning of my hurt, what am I doing wrong, and what am I to get out of this?

I know without God there is no life, and I know God is in my heart, but my spirit cries out. What am I to do?

I do know that if it had not been for his grace and mercy, I would have not made it thus far.

Has God forgotten about me?

Has his love failed me? I'm so hurt and ashamed of my actions.

Why not now, if there's ever been a time to move forward, is my work in vain?

Surely, the Father sees and hears all. Answer me Lord lest I be like those who turn to utter darkness.

My soul thirsts for redemption. Is it not thee who redeems man from destruction?

I pray every night before I go to sleep and awake and still nothing has changed.

How long, oh Lord, will you allow those to laugh at my shame? How long will the wicked be allowed to do whatever, how long, how long?

For we all are made of dust, and all labor under the sun.

Whether you're Jewish, Catholic, Baptist, Protestant, Mormon, Muslim, Seventh-day Adventist, Jehovah's Witness, or Christian.

These are the many different religions, beliefs, or points of view, so many views on the method of living life. Even if you're an atheist or just don't care, in the end, we all receive a certificate of death.

I'm reminded of the preaching, "All is vanity for a fool has no understanding, the righteous has no fault, but God's grace is extended to all." How long, how long, oh Lord, will you allow me to suffer?

What is the purpose of gifts if we are not able to unlock such talents?

Is this not vanity?

Politics, Politicians, Government, Republicans, Democrats, Independents, Socialist/ Liberal, Revolution, Conservative, Tea party, Far Right, Far Left, Fanatics, Rich, Middle Class, and Poor, whether or not they cut taxes, raise taxes, or do nothing at all.

White, Black, and Brown, Red, White, and Blue, colors of many faces, colors of a Great Nation. Wars of

Violence, Suffering, Poverty, Sickness, Disease, Mindless, Thoughtful, Forgiving, and the many dysfunctional ways of mankind, Brotherhood, Sisterhood, and our Traditional Family Values.

Hurt, Pain, Sorrow, and Tears of Joy.

One Nation, one people, one voice, and the endless sound of rivers overflowing. Earth, wind, fire, peace, love, hate, and the horror of bodies without movement, is it all useless?

Is all work in vain?

Vanity of vanities, saith the preacher; all is vanity. And moreover, because the preacher was wise, he still taught the people knowledge; yea, he gave good heed, and sought out, and set in order many proverbs. The preacher sought to find out acceptable words: and that which was written was upright, even words of truth; the words of the wise, are as goads and as nails fastened by the masters of assemblies, which are given from one shepherd. And further, by these, my son, be admonished: of making many books there is no end; and much study is a weariness of the flesh. Let us hear the conclusion of the whole matter: Fear God, and keep his commandments: for this is the whole duty of man.

> For God, shall bring every work into judgment, with every secret thing, whether it is good, or whether it is evil.
>
> Ecclesiastes 12:8–14 (KJV)

The Prayers

How do we know if God answers prayers?

Why do my prayers take so long to be answered?

Are only the people who are living their lives according to God, are their prayers answered?

Why can't I hear the voice of God when I pray?

Why can't I feel anything when I pray to God?

Which kind of prayers does God answer or do my prayers fall on deaf ears?

Well, there are many ways to explaining this.

I've felt these same feelings as well and found myself questioning God, not knowing that God heard everything I prayed about, but isn't that something, how we allow ourselves or deceive ourselves into thinking God doesn't hear us.

The enemy is quick to try and deceive us as if God doesn't hear us, and we go right along in believing this lie.

Well, I would like to share something with you and let you know that God does hear, and he does answer not only the prayers of the righteous, but also, those of us who are struggling with staying obedient to his will, and God answers our prayers not on our time, but God's time, for the Lord ways work.

I'm reminded of the scripture:

> And when he had opened the seventh seal, there was silence in heaven about the space of half an hour and I saw the seven angels which stood before God; and to them were given seven trumpets. And another angel came and stood at the altar, having a golden censer; and there was given unto him much incense, that he should offer it with the prayers of all saints upon the golden altar which was before the throne.
>
> Revelation 8:1–3 (KJV)

I believe and know this to be true even at the time of prayer, when we feel as if God is not talking back to us through our prayers, he hears us, and he will give you his answer in due time. God loves it when we come to him in prayer and wants to give us everything we ask for.

Please understand that God does take care of those who love him and calls on his name. It is our sins that keep God from doing more in our lives, and the enemy knows this; that's why the enemy tries so hard to keep us in sin, in order to keep us from experiencing God's favor in our lives.

The children of Israel prayed to be freed from their Egyptian masters, and when the time or season was right, it came to pass, but by their disobedience or sin, they did not experience or receive the full benefit of their prayers.

When we go to God in prayer and we are sincere about changing our lives and not just because we want something from God, when we ask him, we will see it come to pass. Even in our disobedience, the Lord still answers our prayers.

> He hath not dealt with us after our sins; nor rewarded us according to our iniquities. For as the heaven is high above the earth, so great is his mercy toward them that fear him. As far as the east is from the west, so far hath he removed our transgressions from us. Like as a father, pitieth his children, so the Lord pitieth them that fear him. For he knoweth our frame; he remembereth we are dust.
>
> Psalm 103:10–15 (KJV)

> Jesus Christ is the same, yesterday, today and forever.
>
> Hebrews 13:8 (NLT)

Heaven

Imagine gardens blooming with life, streams of rivers that flow constantly and never dry up, a place of no more pain, a place of peace and joy, where all walks of life come together, no more hate, sickness, or disease, a place that allows us to be totally free from stress, worrying, and death itself, a place where darkness does not exist, where spiritual beings rule the skyline, and angels sing praises to the Most High God.

Imagine a place that has no ending, where love is unconditional, and the air is without pollution.

Imagine a place where there is no void that exists, a place where tears are as foreign as the word itself and walking in love, in God's love, is an everyday occurrence.

This place called heaven is the final destination of the believer, for all who follow after God's way of life while living here on earth.

Imagine being able to walk and talk with Jesus, everything we ever hoped for, everything we believed, asking God himself about everything, seeing all those who came before us and died in Jesus's name. Can you imagine that?

What an awesome and marvelous time it will be for those of us who have waited patiently to see the Kingdom of God.

We ourselves will now be made new, receiving new bodies that are immune to sickness, disease, and death. Can you imagine the Glory of God?

Jesus tells us that in his Father's house are many mansions:

> If it were not so, I would have told you. I go to prepare a place for you; and if I go and prepare a place for you, I will come again, and receive you unto myself; that where I am, there ye may be also.
>
> John 14:2–3 (KJV)

Isn't that wonderful? Christ assures us, no, He guarantees us a spot in the kingdom of heaven. When we open up our hearts to Jesus and follow after the ways of the Eternal God, we will be seated with Christ in Heaven.

I pray for us all to make it in God's eternal kingdom. Amen.

Faith Without Works

Have you ever asked yourself, what the meaning of operating in faith is? And if so, that's okay for we've all questioned someone or something one time or another. Even in this day in time, man still questions their own existence as if we were the evolution of something other than God.

I guess if you tell yourself something over and over, you start to believe whatever you want or tame your mind to it.

Likewise, how can one say they love God and there is no action behind their words for love is an action word, which is the fact or process and requires something being done?

Scripture tells or asks us:

> What doth it profit, my brethren, though a man say he hath faith, and have not works? Can faith save him? If a brother or sister be naked, and destitute of daily food, and one of you say unto them, depart in peace, be ye warmed and filled; notwithstanding ye give them not those things which are needful to the body; what doth it profit? Even so faith, if it hath not works, is dead, being alone. Yea, a man may say, thou hast faith, and I have works: show me thy faith without thy works, and I will show thee my faith by my works. Thou believest that there is one God; thou does well: the devils also believe, and tremble.
>
> James 2:14–19 (KJV)

> But wilt thou know, O vain man, that faith without works is dead? Was not Abraham our father justified by works, when he had offered Isaac his son upon the altar? See thou how faith wrought with his works and by works was faith made perfect? And the scripture was fulfilled which said, Abraham believed God, and it was imputed unto him for righteousness: and he was called the Friend of God. Ye see then how that by works a man is justified, and not by faith only. Likewise also was not Rahab the harlot justified by works, when she had received the messengers, and had sent them out another way, for as the body without the spirit, is dead, so faith without works, is dead also.
>
> James 2:20–26 (KJV)

This not only lets us know that faith without works is dead, but it backs it up with scripture. Once we come into the understanding and obedience of the Word of God, our Faith shall sustain us, but our works will determine our outcome.

We must know that just going to Bible study or church is only a small portion of the puzzle.

Remember, Christ and the apostles roamed the countryside, spreading the Good News of God.

May God bless you as you go about carrying God's message to the world?

Know Your Enemy

We as believers, whether new beginners or a believer for many years, must know the enemy we face for the enemy knows you and I by name and goes to and fro, seeking to devour whom he may.

His plan is to kill, steal, and destroy us who love the Lord. God has protected us from this tyrant for many years, and we who accept Jesus Christ are covered by the shedding of his blood at Calvary.

But what is the true origin of the enemy or what do some call him by? Which is his other name, that old devil or serpent Lucifer?

There are various religious documents that detail the fall of Satan or Lucifer, which are one and the same, and sheds light on his downfall from God's Grace.

Lucifer was very resentful of his role to God and led a failed rebellion against the Almighty God, which ended up in him being banished from heaven.

This is how Satan, the devil, earned many of his names. The book of Isaiah refers to him as a fallen star known as Lucifer. Although he is banished from the kingdom of God, he takes a third of the angels with him; this third of angels joined Lucifer in his rebellion against righteousness, against God. Can you picture a third of the angels rebelling against God? What madness!

Whether Christian, Jewish, or Muslim, all three religions do agree that the reason Satan was banished from heaven was because of his arrogance and disobedience, which brought him into conflict with God.

Lucifer, preying on God's creation, which is mankind, has used evil tactics against man as his revenge against God. So what motivates this being to rebel against God's wonderful love?

I think we all know the answer to that for we deal with these deadly temptations on the regular. Pride, envy, and lust have kept us all in bondage, and that's just three of many.

We, being created in God's perfect love, we choose not to rebel purposely like our adversary, the devil, but through Jesus Christ, we go to God on bended knee, asking for his forgiveness. Not so the enemy, for Satan, he wants to destroy you and I and see if he can compete for the souls of men, women, and children. Such an evil force we are up against.

> And every spirit that confesseth not that Jesus Christ is come in the flesh is not of God: and this is that spirit of antichrist, whereof ye have heard that it should come; and even now already is it in the world.
>
> 1 John 4:3 (KJV)

The Antichrist is the enemy of Christ who will spread evil throughout the world before being conquered at Christ's Second Coming.

Satan is also believed to increase his power through weaponry and trickery, through shape-shifting to poses or inhabit other beings to do his dirty deeds.

The devil and his demons of evil, work together in trying to divide and conquer or devour what God has made.

The enemy comes to us in many different forms. His most boldly act was when he came to Eve in the garden as a serpent. The enemy tries to lure mankind from its Creator in hopes of winning our souls as he prepares for what is called the end of days.

Most scholars believe that the snake, then, which is to be a manifestation of Satan, tempted Eve to eat the fruit from the tree of knowledge, which was forbidden by God, thus this sparked the fall of man, for after Eve ate from the tree, Adam did so as well.

The Garden of Eden is believed to be the first attack of Satan, unleashing his evilness against mankind. This was the beginning of many attacks to come and still holds fast today. We see it all too well in humanity.

In the Old Testament book of Job, we see Satan at best doing what he believes to be victorious in trying to break Job's spirit. Although Job wavered a little and started asking God why this bad stuff was happening to him, in the end, Job did not renounce God and received his reward.

The ancient writings of Christians, Jews, and Muslims all share the idea of a divine emissary to lead the charge against the forces of evil as this will be the final conflict between good versus evil, and we as Christians or followers of Christ can be assured by God's Word that we have the Victory.

May God's peace come upon all of us who diligently seek him?

Scriptures of Need

God's presence and power......................Exodus 4:17 (KJV)
How to pray.....................................Matthew 6:5–6 (KJV)
The Lord's Prayer............................Matthew 6:9–13 (KJV)
Backsliding ....James 5:19–20 (KJV)
God on your side ....Deuteronomy 3:21–22 (KJV)
Forgiveness of sin........................2 Samuel 12:20–24 (KJV)
Righteousness ....Genesis 15:6 (KJV)
Courage ....Psalm 18:30 (KJV)
Believers ....Romans 8:9 (KJV)
Bitterness.. Genesis 33:1–11 (KJV)
Blame ....1 Samuel 30:6 (KJV)
Blessings .... 2 kings 5:9–15 (KJV)
Jesus Blood ....Matthew 26:28 (KJV)
Promise to Noah.......................... Genesis 9:8–17 (KJV)
Healing... Matthew 15:29–31 (KJV)
Faithfulness.......................................Luke 23:39–43 (KJV)
Family...Psalm 128 (KJV)
Sickness .... Matthew 4:23–24 (KJV)
Desires..............................1 Thessalonians 4:1–8 (2) (KJV)
Sin ....Colossians 2:13–15 (KJV)
Removing the things which
causes us to sin...........................Matthew 18:8–9 (KJV)

Victory....................................1 Samuel 4:5–8 (KJV)
Victory.......................................Ephesians 4:8 (KJV)
Victory..............................Hebrews 11:32–35 (KJV)
Victory...1 John 3:8–9 (KJV)

The scriptures tell us that

> my people are being destroyed for lack of knowledge because they don't know me.
>
> Hosea 4:6 (NLT)

This is the reason why a lot of us who start out on the right track either fall to the wayside or just don't make it at all.

Let this day be your day of really getting to know God. For those of us who build a personal relationship with God will understand his truths about living the life that he has for us.

There is a whole new world for those who choose the Lord's way of life, and your eyes will be opened to so many wonderful things as you get to know God.

The Lord protects, he guides, he watches, he heals, he supplies, he comforts, he forgives, he has mercy, and he brings justice to all who are oppressed.

> For the Lord is good; his mercy is everlasting; and his truth endureth to all generations.
>
> Psalm 100:5 (KJV)

The Test

Tests are an everyday occurrence that try and hinder us in our spiritual and natural lives. You may find yourself going through different test all throughout the day.

Whether on the job with co-workers or management or maybe it's the boss, or the loss of a job, or at home with the kids, maybe its food, candy, chocolate, it's sometimes amazing to me, how we are not discipline enough to stop eating what we know too be bad for our health, or maybe its drugs and alcohol, pornography, family members, or maybe it's friends we may need to move on from.

The tests we face can range from the smallest thing to a giant battle. What may be small to some may be big in someone else's life.

Here are some more examples of tests we face when we're trying to live our lives accordingly to our Christian Faith.

The kids leaving the ice tray empty, or the lid off of the jar of peanut butter, the kids not doing there chores, the baby keeps crying, dad's in a bad mood or vice versa, or mom doesn't do this and dad doesn't do that, toothpaste in the sink, there are just to many to name them all, but I know you get the point.

Then there are the big tests, like cigarettes, prescription drugs, street drugs, alcohol, or adultery, also the loss of a loved one, a friend's betrayal, or rejection, or maybe you're faced with depression, anxiety, health, homeless, or just dealing with everyday situations.

The Devil/ The Enemy knows what gets us off track and knows how to set us up to get irritated with things or people in order to steal our joy and he tries his best to separate us from the love of God.

I too find myself going through much of the same mess over and over and over, wondering if I will be able to defeat this test that keeps plaguing away at my soul.

Why are we going through much of the same mess over and over and over again and again?

Defeating these test are only as hard as we make them. The reason I believe we keep going through, and I know we all differ, is because we're not trusting and leaning on God in the way we ought to. I say this again; so that you want forget it. I know you pray and worship God, attend church on the regular, bible study, etc…

It is when faced with these tests that we need to understand, not why, but what's the purpose or the trickery of the enemy to get us off track and not give into the temptation.

Do not lose your temper, do not spiral out of control, or become frustrated, and do not let pride or your feelings overtake you. You have all the control; all you have to do is speak it.

Have you ever noticed, when you're in a deep thought or your mind is thinking of a number of things and if someone interrupts you, it breaks up your train of thought.

So when faced with temptation try calling on the name of Jesus, speak it out loud, yell it if you have to and watch how it breaks up that thought of temptation and repeat the process over and over again until you claim your victory. Remember, you already have the victory; all you need to do is speak it, receive it, claim it, because it is already done.

Have you ever wondered why those of us who do fail the test, or allow sin to dwell in our minds and hearts, how you feel so apologetic, and all the day you may go through praying to God for forgiveness, the reason being is because of your conscious understanding what your spirit knows to be wrong, but smile, because you're now starting to take notice, or be self-aware of the tests that the opposition tries to put in front of you and also, you're more alert to the sin in your life.

Remember there were times when some of the things we did or people we hurt didn't bother us, only when God's Holy Spirit came upon us did we truly feel sorry for our actions.

This is how we start winning or passing the test, by applying our God-given ability, which is spending time with the Lord, having a real relationship with him, studying, believing, and trusting in Jesus Christ, also walking in love, which covers a multitude of sin. Hatred stirreth up strifes: but love covereth all sins (Proverbs 10:12 KJV).

God has given those us who follow after his ways the manuscript on how to withstand the test and sin that comes our way.

I found that in my walk, I would ask God to remind me of every time, when faced with tests, that he or his Holy Spirit, to give me the strength, not to give in, to temptation or not to give a negative response to something or someone, who or what, may be the sole purpose to distract me from staying on course.

I do know God does answer prayers, and it was at that moment that a test was staring me right in the face. I got up and looked in the mirror and said to myself, now what are you going to do.

Here I was going back and forth about going on the internet and going on sites that I know God would not be pleased about, and I don't just mean adult sites, any websites or blogs that were not lined up with the word of God. Things such as music, gossip, etc…

I had a very uneasy feeling in my spirit, for I knew that I was going to give into the temptation. I was so hurt and disgusted with myself and I asked God to forgive me a thousand times over, only to give in a couple of days later to watching one of my favorite shows on cable television (Spartacus), which is based on the history of the Roman society and their dominance in the land at that time. I love anything pertaining to the history of mankind, and how the people and land has changed over the centuries.

Although I love the show there is just too much nudity and strong sexual content being exposed? We must be on guard all the time in what we put in our spirit, the things we observe on television, things we listen to and speak out of our mouths.

Well, little did I know, God already knew what I was going to do, before I knew, what I was going to do, but even in the time of turmoil God makes a way for us to escape it, as I sat there going back and forth, I could hear in my Spirit the Lord reminding me of what I asked him to do and that's the part that made me sick. Here I was struggling, and the fact that God kept his part and I did not keep mine, by leaning on him, and calling out to him, made me feel horrible. God's pleasure goes way beyond that of the pleasures we feel here in the natural.

Take diamonds or luxury cars/trucks, nice homes, exotic foods or perfumes, just any pleasures of the world and combine them all in one and still that's no comparison to God's pleasure or favor we as followers of Christ will experience.

Well, it took a lot of patience and me rededicating myself to spending time with God on an everyday basis, as if I was going to work. Making God the first thing I give my time to and prayer, fasting, praising and practicing the ways of our Lord and Savior Jesus Christ.

Remember scripture lets us know?

> There hath no temptation taken you but such as is common to man: but God is faithful, who will not suffer you to be tempted above that ye are able; but will with the temptation also make a way to escape, that ye may be able to bear it.
>
> 1 Corinthians 10:13 (KJV)

I also love the way the Amplified version puts it.

> For no temptation (no trial regarded as enticing to sin), [no matter how it comes or where it leads] has overtaken you that is not common to man [that is, no temptation or trial has come to you that is beyond human resistance and that is not adjusted and adapted and belonging to human experience, and such as man can bear]. But God is faithful [to His Word and His compassionate nature], and He [can be trusted] not to let you be tempted and tried and assayed beyond your ability and strength of resistance and power to endure, but with the temptation He will [always] also provide the way out (the means of escape to a landing place), that you may be capable and strong and powerful to bear up under it patiently.
>
> 1 Corinthians 10:13 (AMP)

The Israelites started out on an eleven day journey which ended up lasting forty years in the wilderness.

How does an eleven-day trip turn into a forty-year journey?

Let us look at what the scripture says.

> And thou shalt remember all the way which the Lord thy God led thee these forty years in the wilderness, to humble thee and prove thee, to know what was in thine heart, whether thou wouldest keep his commandments, or no.
>
> Deuteronomy 8:2 (KJV)

We as people of Faith shall be tested, but we have confidence in him which is Jesus Christ who went to the Cross for you and I, promised us that we will prevail.

What Scripture tells us, in that?

> These things I have spoken unto you, that in me ye might have peace. In the world ye shall have tribulation: but be of good cheer; I have overcome the world.
>
> John 16:33 (KJV)

We must stay steadfast in the Lord, guard our mouths, because I know we've all said or did things in our past or even present that we probably are not proud of. We must take control of our lives and I know this can be hard, because I do know things happen out of the blue sometimes or unexpectedly, but with God's ability on our ability there is nothing that can stand against us, all power onto the Most High God who gives us the strength to overcome.

> My brethren, count it all joy when ye fall into divers temptations; Knowing this, that the trying of your faith worketh patience.
>
> James 1:2-3 (KJV)

> Consider it wholly joyful, my brethren, whenever you are enveloped in or encounter trials of any sort or fall into various temptations. Be assured and understand that the trial and proving of your faith bring out endurance and steadfastness and patience.
>
> James 1:2-3 (AMP)

> Blessed is the man that endureth temptation: for when he is tried, he shall receive the crown of life, which the Lord hath promised to them that love him.
>
> James 1:12 (KJV)

> Blessed (happy, to be envied) is the man who is patient under trial and stands up under temptation, for when he has stood the test and been approved, he will receive [the victor's] crown of life which God has promised to those who love him.
>
> James 1:12 (AMP)

Gospel Truths

Let not your heart be troubled; ye believe in God, believe also in me. In my Father's house are many mansions: if it were not so, I would have told you. I go to prepare a place for you. And if I go and prepare a place for you, I will come again, and receive you unto myself; that where I am, there ye may be also. And whither I go ye know, and the way ye know. Thomas saith unto him, Lord, we know not whither thou goes; and how can we know the way? Jesus saith unto him, I am the way, the truth, and the life: no man cometh unto the Father, but by me. If ye had known me, ye should have known my Father also: and from henceforth ye know him, and have seen him.

John 14:1–7 (KJV)

Philip said unto him, show us the Father and it sufficeth us. Jesus saith unto him, have I been so long time with you, and yet hast thou not known me, Philip? He that hath seen me hath seen the Father; and how says thou then, show us the Father? Believe thou not that I am in the Father, and the Father in me? The words that I speak unto you I speak not of myself: but the Father that dwells in me, he does the works. Believe me that I am in the

Father, and the Father in me: or else believe me for the very works' sake.

John 14:8–11 (KJV)

Believe it or not, this is what separates Christian believers from other religions, for we believe that Jesus is Lord.

The Trinity—God the Father—God the Son—God the Holy Spirit.

It's time for Christians all over the world to stand up and confess that Jesus is Lord and not feel threatened by doing so.

May this book be a blessing to all who read it and give you a better account of what God wants for your life? Amen.